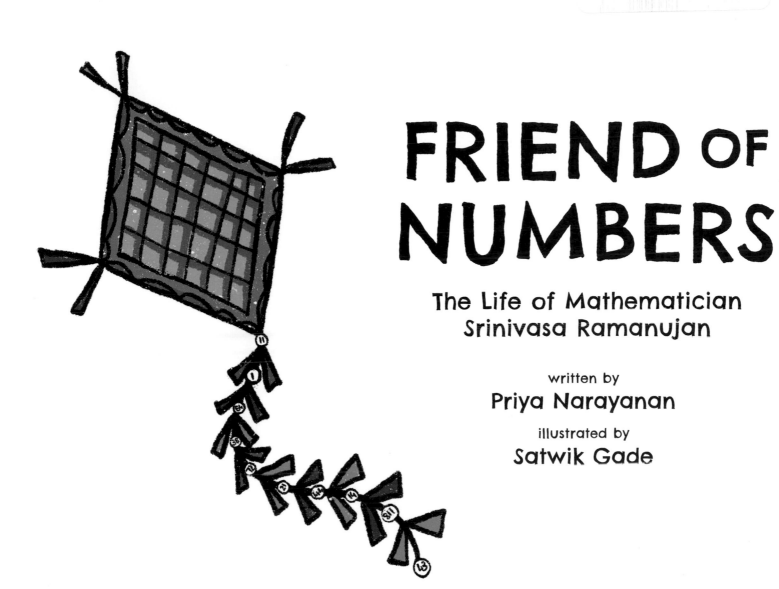

FRIEND OF NUMBERS

The Life of Mathematician Srinivasa Ramanujan

written by
Priya Narayanan

illustrated by
Satwik Gade

Eerdmans Books for Young Readers

Grand Rapids, Michigan

Priya Narayanan is a writer, poet, and interior architect based in Ahmedabad, India. While researching *Friend of Numbers*, she traveled to many places associated with Srinivasa Ramanujan, including his homes in Kumbakonam and Chennai, India, and in Cambridge, England. Visit Priya's website at priyanarayanan.in and follow her on Twitter @moonspotting.

Satwik Gade is an artist and designer whose work is inspired by comics, Indian mythology, and Impressionist art. He lives in Chennai, India, where he is a political cartoonist for the newspaper *The Hindu*. Follow Satwik on Instagram @satwikgade.

Text © 2019 Priya Narayanan
Illustrations © 2019 Satwik Gade
Originally published in English as *Srinivasa Ramanujan: Friend of Numbers*
© 2019 Tulika Publishers, Chennai, India

First published in the United States in 2023
by Eerdmans Books for Young Readers,
an imprint of Wm. B. Eerdmans Publishing Co.
Grand Rapids, Michigan
www.eerdmans.com/youngreaders

Manufactured in China

32 31 30 29 28 27 26 25 24 23   1 2 3 4 5 6 7 8 9

ISBN 978-0-8028-5608-1

A catalog record of this book is available from the Library of Congress.

Illustrations created digitally.

The author's note, glossary, and mathematical content were created
in collaboration with the author for the Eerdmans edition of this book.

MIX
Paper | Supporting
responsible forestry
FSC® C104723

It was the 22nd of December in 1887. The weather was pleasant, and the mighty Kaveri River meandered as usual toward the sea along its tree-lined banks near the city of Erode. Just after sunset, a boy was born to Srinivasa and Komalam.

Ten days later, in keeping with tradition, he was given a name—Srinivasa Iyengar Ramanujan.

Soon after, the family moved back to Kumbakonam, where Ramanujan's father worked as a clerk at a sari shop. Ramanujan grew up a quiet little boy, always thinking, always full of questions.

How far away are the clouds?

How big are the stars?

How long is the equator?

But most of all, he was fascinated by numbers.

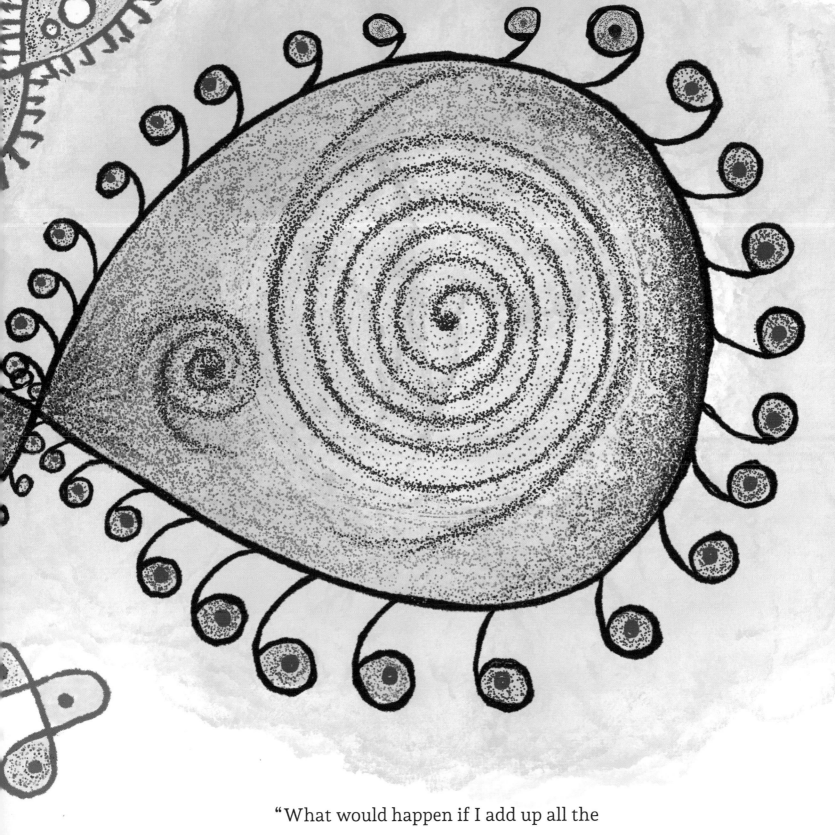

"What would happen if I add up all the numbers in the world?" he'd wonder.

"Is it even possible to do that?"

"Is there a LAST number?"

Every morning, as his mother gave him a bath,
Ramanujan would watch the ripples in the water
move outwards in circles, from small to big.

As she combed his long hair and coiled it into a knot, he would
hear chants from the temple nearby—*namah somaya, somaya
namo . . . namah somaya cha, cha somaya namo . . .*

And as she walked him to school, he would look up at the rows of gods and goddesses carved on the temple gopurams.

There were patterns all around him. Were there patterns in numbers too?

As he grew up, while other children played games on the street after school, Ramanujan played with numbers.

He sat with his slate and chalk, filling the slate with numbers, rubbing them out with his elbow and starting again. Numbers tossed and turned in front of him. They came together, and they moved apart.

They made patterns

only he could see.

Seeing him lost in thought, the other children would sneak up behind him to push pebbles down his dhoti. When he got up, the pebbles fell with a clatter. The others clapped and laughed, but Ramanujan just went back to thinking.

When Ramanujan was ten years old, his teacher said in class:

"If you divide any number by itself, you will get 1. For example, if you divide 3 fruits among 3 people, each will get 1."

Ramanujan wasn't sure. "Sir, what if no fruits are divided among no people? How will anyone get 1?"

The teacher was astonished. This wasn't a question an ordinary child would ask!

When Ramanujan was older, he was gifted a book with thousands of mathematical problems. Excited, he worked at them, forgetting everything else.

"You're wasting your time!" his father said angrily.

But Ramanujan couldn't stop. He worked on the problems, hiding under the only bed in their house.

By the time he reached the end of the book, he was obsessed.

There were so many types of numbers—odd, even, whole, fractional, prime, composite...

Like an artist exploring forms and colors or a poet exploring words and images, Ramanujan threw himself into exploring numbers.

Soon he lost interest in all other subjects. Every time he opened his English or history book, numbers sneaked and slunk into the pages.

They made patterns only he could see.

Not surprisingly, he failed all his college exams except mathematics. Hoping that Ramanujan might mend his ways, his parents got him married to Janaki, a quiet girl much younger than he was. He now realized he needed a job and got one as a clerk. His parents were upset because it was low-paying, but Ramanujan was happy to have free time to work on his ideas.

When he showed these to senior mathematicians, they were impressed. "Your work is good!" they said, and helped him publish some of them.

Ramanujan did not want to remain simply "good." He wanted to get better. So he wrote to three well-known mathematics professors at England's Cambridge University, asking to join them, to learn more from them.

In their eyes, Ramanujan was only a clerk from a faraway colony of the British Empire. Could his strange ideas and equations really be important? Two of the professors said, "No."

But Professor Godfrey Hardy saw a spark of something special in Ramanujan. "Come and work with me!" he wrote back.

Ramanujan was thrilled, but also anxious. Back in those days, Brahmins like him were forbidden to travel overseas.

"Will relatives invite me to their homes again?" he worried. "Will friends remain friends? Will I still be allowed to pray to Goddess Namagiri in her temple?"

Then he remembered what his mother had always told him: "Listen to your heart's voice and be strong enough to do what it says."

So he prepared to go to England. Before the journey, though, many changes awaited him that he did not like at all!

Once at Cambridge, Ramanujan quickly threw himself into his mathematical work. He was happy in his world where numbers tumbled about, falling into patterns.

Sometimes Professor Hardy saw these patterns too, and was glad he had asked Ramanujan to come. Under his guidance, Ramanujan wrote several papers that were published in important journals, and soon...

"Who is this bright-eyed genius from India?" everyone wanted to know.

In the meantime, World War I had reached its peak. Many left Cambridge, either to join war services or move to safer towns. Air raids after dark forced people to remain indoors.

Ramanujan missed the nightlong discussions with friends that he was so used to. Feeling homesick, he wanted to return to India, but it wasn't safe to travel.

There was gloom all around him, and there was gloom within him. The only thing that kept him going was his love for numbers.

Shut in his room, Ramanujan worked on new ideas as numbers continued to dance around him.

They made patterns

only he could see.

One evening, as Ramanujan was getting ready to make some rasam, a few lentils fell on the table—7, he counted.

"How many ways can I arrange them?" he suddenly wondered.

Soon, he was making combinations of lentils that added up to 7.

By the time he finished, Ramanujan had counted 15 different combinations. Curious, he tried the same with larger numbers of lentils—8, 9, 10, 11...

It was well past midnight when Ramanujan discovered that he could make 627 different combinations of lentils that added to 20. By then, there were lentils all over—on the table, floor, stove, sofa, and even his bed.

And the rasam was still not made!

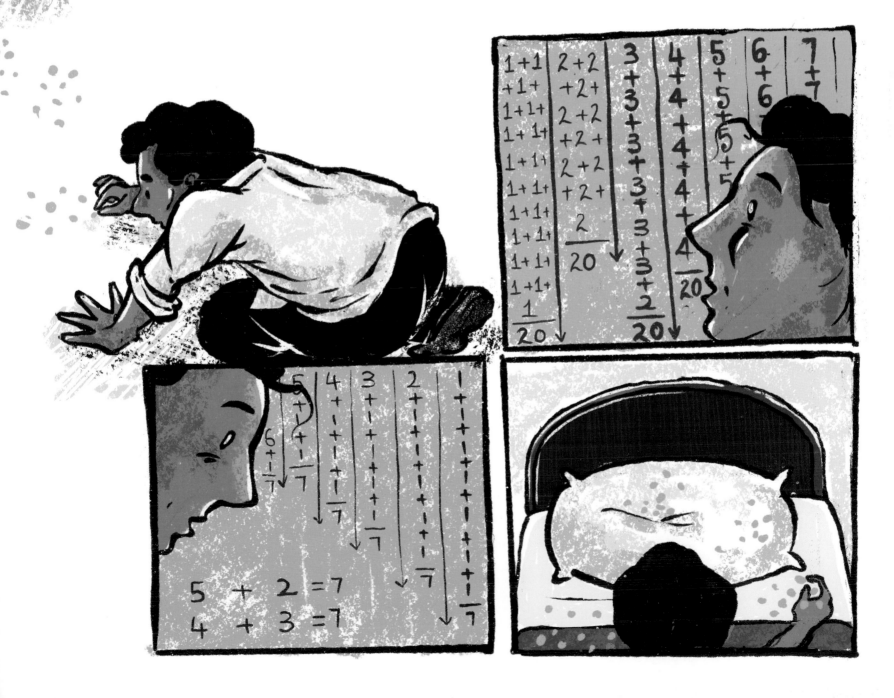

Ramanujan couldn't sleep all night. "Can I find a way to calculate how many different ways smaller numbers can be added up to get the same large number?" he thought.

Early next morning, he rushed to Professor Hardy. The two immersed themselves in discussions that led to some very important discoveries.

Another day, Professor Hardy happened to mention that the taxi he had just come in had quite a boring number—1729.

"No! It is a very interesting number," Ramanujan shot back. His sharp memory drew out something he'd read about long ago, and on a piece of paper he scribbled:

$$1729 = (12 \times 12 \times 12) + (1 \times 1 \times 1)$$
$$1729 = (10 \times 10 \times 10) + (9 \times 9 \times 9)$$

"Look at the pattern!" he exclaimed.

Numbers were his friends. He could remember special things about them, the way that one remembers a friend's birthday.

The cold Cambridge weather and lack of vegetarian food made Ramanujan fall ill often. But that didn't stop him from working. If his hospital room became too cold, he worked for hours at a time in the much warmer bathroom.

In 1919, though, his health got worse.

The war had ended by now, so Ramanujan could return to India to be in the care and comfort of his family. His doctors, however, weren't sure he would recover.

Even as he grew weaker, all Ramanujan could think of was numbers. Lying in bed, his head propped up on pillows, numbers swirled and twirled in his mind.

They made patterns only he could see...

. . . patterns that he scribbled on sheets of paper until his very last breath.

Ramanujan passed away on April 26, 1920, when he was only 32. In that short time, he not only worked with his beloved numbers to make important contributions to mathematics, he also fulfilled his childhood curiosity by calculating the length of the equator to be 40,078 km. Today, it has taken us calculators and computers to know that the length is around 40,075 km!

The thousands of ideas that Ramanujan left behind also continue to help scientists understand how the universe began, how black holes behave, how computers—and even the internet—can work better, how cancer treatment can be improved, and so much more.

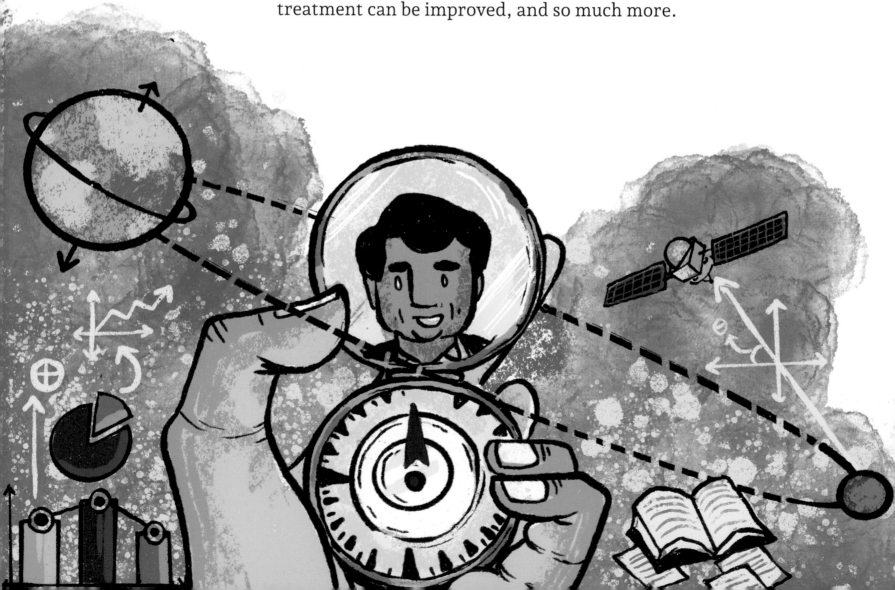

AUTHOR'S NOTE

More than 130 years ago, when India was still under British rule, people traveled mostly by animal carts, buses, and trains, and used ships to travel abroad, not airplanes. Electronic handheld calculators (let alone computers) had not yet been invented, so one had to use reams and reams of paper to do mathematical calculations. It was against this background that a bright-eyed boy named Srinivasa Ramanujan grew up to become an important, world-renowned mathematician.

Although Ramanujan, the mathematician, has long been a beloved figure in India, with his face on postage stamps and his birthday celebrated as National Mathematics Day, not many Indians know about Ramanujan, the person. Even mathematicians and scientists living abroad who work with Ramanujan's ideas do not know much about his life story. I myself first learned about the finer details of the life and times of Ramanujan only in 2016, and only through the work of a foreigner, Robert Kanigel.

Kanigel's full-length book *The Man who Knew Infinity* had me hooked from the first page to the last. Even as I was reading it, I asked myself why there was no book on Ramanujan by an Indian author. More importantly, while there were many fascinating biographies of western scientists to inspire children, why wasn't there much on Ramanujan for a young audience?

Soon after I finished reading that book, I got an opportunity to go to Chennai (known as Madras during Ramanujan's time), which is nearly 1,800 km (1,200 miles) away from my city. Since Kumbakonam, Ramanujan's hometown, was only an overnight train ride away from Chennai, I decided on an impulse to make that extra journey.

Once in Kumbakonam, I strolled up and down the street that once witnessed the many eccentricities of the young Ramanujan. I marveled at the massive gopuram of the Sarangapani temple, as little Ramanujan would have, strained my ears to catch the Vedic chants being recited within the temple, and sat on the high plinth of his house where he spent hours with a slate and chalk, working on his mathematical ideas. Inside the house, I peered under the cot where he hid himself to solve equations away from his father's disapproving eyes, ran my hands through the vessels in the kitchen that Ramanujan would line up against the wall for fun, and dipped my fingers in the water from the backyard well where his mother drew his bathwater every day. In every nook and cranny of the house, I heard whispers of Ramanujan's childhood, a story waiting to be written.

Back home, as I was reading up about Ramanujan's mathematical ideas, I came across the Ramanujan summation:

$$1 + 2 + 3 + \cdots + \infty = -1/12$$

The equation had left even his mentor G. H. Hardy flummoxed at first glance, so you can imagine what it did to a non-mathematical brain like mine! I knew then that to understand Ramanujan, the person, I would have to understand the mathematician too. I'm grateful to Mokshay Madiman, a high school friend who is now a mathematics professor and researcher at the University of Delaware, for taking the time to explain the meaning of the equation over two engrossing hours.

A year later, another friend, Dr. Murali Narasimhan, helped me find two houses in Chennai where Ramanujan had briefly stayed as a young man. The first was a modest one-room house in Triplicane where he lived before leaving for Cambridge; the second was a magnificent villa belonging to a rich patron where he stayed in 1919, just before his death. The contrasting nature of these houses showed me how much Ramanujan's stature had grown in the eyes of India's scientific community within just a few years.

In 2019, ninety-nine years after Ramanujan's death, I got an opportunity to travel to London for work. Consumed by my desire to understand the mathematical genius better, I stole out time to visit all the places in England where Ramanujan had stayed. I was lucky to get connected with Richard Chapling, a young professor at Trinity College, Cambridge, where Ramanujan had worked with Hardy. Together, we visited the house on Cromwell Road where Ramanujan had stayed when he first arrived in London and the Putney house where he had the taxicab number conversation with Hardy.

At Cambridge, Richard enthusiastically showed me around Trinity College, including the iconic Wren Library, the majestic dining hall, and the chapel where Ramanujan's name has been immortalized alongside other world-famous Trinity alumni like Sir Isaac Newton. We later walked across the Great Court to the block in Bishop's Hostel where the "rasam incident" in this book took place. As we strolled the streets of Cambridge and punted along the River Cam, Richard kindly explained several of Ramanujan's ideas to me in simple language.

Upon returning home from this trip, I was able to better appreciate the magnitude of what Ramanujan had achieved—from being a poor, superstitious Brahmin boy in an ordinary dusty town in British-occupied southern India, to being acknowledged as one of the world's most brilliant mathematicians. And in all humility, I revised every line of this book so it could do justice not only to Ramanujan's great passion for mathematics, but also to his never-failing innocence and vulnerability as a person.

If I have learned one lesson from Ramanujan's life, it is to follow my passions without swerving away because of what others think or say. Following his trail across India and England to figure this out was a treat for a traveler like me!

PATTERNS IN NUMBERS

Even when he was a child, Ramanujan was fascinated by the patterns that numbers made. Some of these patterns are easy to spot, some rather difficult. For example,

1, 3, 5, 7, 9, 11 . . . is a pattern of odd numbers, while

2, 4, 6, 8, 10, 12 . . . is a pattern of even numbers.

Why are they a pattern? Because:

1. They form a sequence of numbers. (One number can never make a pattern, can it?)

2. They follow a rule. (In the above examples, each number plus 2 gives the next number in the sequence.)

So, you will find that

5, 10, 15, 20, 25 . . .

is a pattern because it is a series that follows the rule of adding 5 to each number.

10, 20, 30, 40, 50 . . .

is a pattern because it is a series that follows the rule of adding 10 to each number.

While you can make hundreds of number patterns by following these two basic principles, you can also discover the rule in any pattern by observing the common change happening throughout.

1, 3, 2, 4, 3, 5, 4, 6, 5 . . .

is a sequence where the rule is to add 2 to the first number, subtract 1 from the second number, and repeat this operation infinitely. The pattern, as you can see, is in the operation applied on consecutive numbers, which is

+ 2 − 1 + 2 − 1 + 2 − 1 . . . .

Even a sequence like

10, 100, 1000, 10000, 100000...

follows a pattern where the rule is to keep increasing the value of the exponent:

$$10, 10^2, 10^3, 10^4, 10^5 \ldots \quad \text{and so on.}$$

LET'S PRACTICE

Can you figure out the patterns in these number sequences? How did you know which number came next?

$$3, 5, 7, 9, \underline{\quad}, \underline{\quad}, \underline{\quad}, \ldots$$

$$77, 73, 69, 65, \underline{\quad}, \underline{\quad}, \underline{\quad}, \ldots$$

$$3, 9, 27, 81, \underline{\quad}, \underline{\quad}, \underline{\quad}, \ldots$$

$$0, 3, 2, 5, 4, 7, 6, 8, \underline{\quad}, \underline{\quad}, \underline{\quad}, \ldots$$

You might have noticed that the more complex the rule, the more interesting the patterns become, and the more difficult it becomes for you to spot the pattern. Once you have mastered and start enjoying these simple patterns, you can move to really complicated ones such as

$$1, 11, 111, 1111 \ldots$$

The rule followed here is

$$1 = 1$$

$$11 = 10 + 1 \ (10^1 + 1)$$

$$111 = 100 + 10 + 1 \ (10^2 + 10^1 + 1)$$

$$1111 = 1000 + 100 + 10 + 1 \ (10^3 + 10^2 + 10^1 + 1) \quad \text{and so on.}$$

Did you notice here that, unlike the previous patterns, the rule does not involve applying mathematical operations on the numbers in the sequence (1, 11, 111, etc.) themselves? Instead, the numbers in the sequence are the result of adding multiples of 10 to 1 in a specific pattern, as indicated in the parentheses. Can you figure out what number comes next in this sequence and why?

MAGIC SQUARES

A magic square is a square grid (or array) of integers (whole numbers) arranged so that the sum of the elements in any column, row, or diagonal is the same. In the grid on the left, every row, column, and diagonal adds up to the same number—36! Now look at the grid on the right—can you use the pattern to fill in the missing numbers?

15	4	17
14	12	10
7	20	9

4	9	2
	5	7
8		

Magic squares have been a part of Indian mathematics since ancient times, when Hindu and Jain astrological scholars constructed different types of magic squares in order to understand planetary positions. However, scholars soon began to construct magic squares for fun, challenging themselves to create bigger and more complex squares through mathematics. Even today, as in Ramanujan's time, magic squares are categorized under "recreational mathematics," which is all about having fun with numbers.

One of the most famous magic squares constructed by Ramanujan was

22	12	18	87
40	65	31	3
71	15	28	25
6	47	62	24

The uniqueness of this square was that the first row is made up of Ramanujan's date of birth: 22/12/1887 (December 22, 1887, written in British style). You will find that all rows, columns, and diagonals in the square add up to 139.

Why don't you try creating a magic square with your own birthday on the first row? Draw a 4x4 grid, write your date of birth on the top row, and find a way to make all the columns, rows, and diagonals add up to the same number.

A GLOSSARY
OF SRINIVASA RAMANUJAN'S WORLD

1729: a "taxicab number," or—as Srinivasa Ramanujan explained—a number expressible as the sum of two cubes (the result of multiplying three instances of n together). Because of Ramanujan and Hardy's conversation about the number's importance, 1729 itself is sometimes known as the Ramanujan number or the Ramanujan-Hardy number.

BRAHMIN: the highest-ranking social caste in Hindu India. In ancient times, Brahmins used to work mostly as temple priests, cooks, teachers, healers, thinkers, writers, and advisors to the royalty. Most of these jobs were low-paying and ensured that despite being the highest in the caste structure, many Brahmins were paradoxically extremely poor. Ordered from highest to lowest social rank, the other castes are: the Kshatriyas (warriors, including the royalty), the Vaishyas (traders and businessmen), and the Shudras (laborers).

Persons belonging to each caste dressed and behaved in a particular way during Ramanujan's time. Consequently, almost everything in his life was informed by his Brahmin identity—the way he dressed, the symbolic *naamam* (caste-mark used by Vaishnavites, or devotees of Lord Vishnu) on his forehead, the tuft of hair on his head, and the vegetarian food he ate. Ramanujan was also highly religious and conscious about his place in the community.

Although the caste system still exists in modern-day India, the nature of work done by the different classes has changed considerably. Also, because the clothing choices of people have changed over the years, it would be very difficult to identify anyone's caste by what they wear.

CAMBRIDGE UNIVERSITY: a research university in Cambridge, England, with a long history of mathematical innovation and study. In March 1916, the university bestowed Srinivasa Ramanujan with a BA (bachelor of arts) through research, on the basis of his paper on highly composite numbers. He was elated. More than twelve years after completing high school and failing his college exams twice, he finally had the much-coveted degree certificate. In 1918 Ramanujan was honored as the second-ever Indian Fellow of the Royal Society and the first-ever Indian Fellow of Trinity College, Cambridge.

DHOTI: a loose garment traditionally worn by men in the Indian subcontinent in response to the hot and dry climate. It is a single long piece of cloth wrapped around the legs and waist and is either knotted in the front or at the back.

ERODE: a South Indian city in the state of Tamil Nadu, located on the banks of the Kaveri River. It is famous for its production of turmeric and textiles.

GODDESS NAMAGIRI: the Hindu goddess Namagiri Thayar of Namakkal. Srinivasa Ramanujan often credited his work to divine revelations from the goddess.

GOPURAM (ALSO GOPURA): a unique feature of South Indian temple architecture, it is a large, impressive gateway monument that marks the entrance of Hindu temples.

IYENGAR: name of a community of Vaishnavite Brahmins belonging to the South Indian state of Tamil Nadu. Members of the community are intensely devoted to Lord Vishnu.

KAVERI: the third-largest river in southern India, which flows across four states before emptying into the Bay of Bengal in east India. The Kaveri is considered sacred and is used to irrigate farms, generate hydroelectric power, and provide water for thousands of households.

KUMBAKONAM: a South Indian city in the state of Tamil Nadu, located in the Kaveri River delta. It is renowned for its ancient Hindu temples, rice cultivation, and filter coffee.

NAMAH SOMAYA, SOMAYA . . . : a Hindu mantra in the "ghanapatha" method of chanting that follows the pattern 1,2,2,1 – 1,2,3,3,2,1 – 1,2,3; 2,3,3,2 – 2,3,4,4,3,2 – 2,3,4 and so on. Since Ramanujan's house was on the temple street, and his mother was highly religious, she would have taken him to the temple to listen to the chants.

RASAM: a light South Indian soup made with spices, ripe tomatoes, tamarind, herbs, and sometimes lentils. Warm and spicy, it is sometimes served to those suffering from coughs or colds.

SARI: a traditional garment worn by women in the Indian subcontinent—a long length of unstitched cloth tied at the waist and draped like a skirt, which then flows around the upper body and over the shoulder.